MW01487379

Crocheters have already fallen in love with Lion Brand's Landscapes® Yarn. The incredible palette of self-striping colors opens the door to creating projects that look like works of art.

The 14 projects showcased in this book use simple shapes and techniques mixed with artful color combinations to take your crochet to the next level.

Explore the endless possibilities of self-striping Landscapes® with these easy-to-make garments and accessories.

About Lion Brand® Yarn Company
Lion Brand® Yarn Company is a 5th generation, family-owned and operated business, and a beloved American brand since 1878. The company is devoted to inspiring and educating knitters and crocheters with yarns, patterns, how-tos, and ideas that elevate their yarn crafting experience.

LEISURE ARTS, INC.
Maumelle, Arkansas

shaded hat and wristers

■□□□ **EASY**

SIZES
Hat
Finished Circumference:
About 19" (48.5 cm), will stretch to fit a range of sizes
Wristers
Finished Circumference:
About 8" (20.5 cm)
Finished Length:
About 6½" (16.5 cm)

SHOPPING LIST
Yarn (Medium Weight) **4 MEDIUM**
LION BRAND® LANDSCAPES®
(Art. #545)
☐ #202 Mountain Range -
2 balls
or color of your choice

Crochet Hooks
LION BRAND® crochet hooks
☐ Size I-9 (5.5 mm)
☐ Size K-10.5 (6.5 mm)
or sizes needed for gauge

Additional Supply
☐ LION BRAND® large-eyed
blunt needle

GAUGE
12 hdc = about 4" (10 cm) with larger hook.
BE SURE TO CHECK YOUR GAUGE.

STITCH GUIDE
HALF DOUBLE CROCHET
2 TOGETHER (abbreviated hdc2tog)
(Yarn over, insert hook in next st and draw up a loop) twice, yarn over and draw through all 5 loops on hook – 1 st decreased.

NOTES
1. Hat and Wristers are each made in one piece in an easy pattern that uses increases and decreases to create diagonal color shading.
2. The first section of Hat and Wristers is shaped with increases and the last section is shaped with decreases. In the center section, an increase is worked at one end and a decrease is worked at the other end of each row.

HAT

With larger hook, ch 3.

Increase Section

Row 1: Work 2 hdc in 3rd ch from hook (2 skipped ch do not count as a st) – you will have 2 hdc in this row.

Row 2: Ch 2 (does not count as a st), turn, 2 hdc in each st – 4 hdc.

Rows 3-15: Ch 2 (does not count as a st), turn, 2 hdc in first st, hdc in each st to last st, 2 hdc in last st – 30 hdc at the end of Row 15.

Center Section

Row 1: Ch 2 (does not count as a st), turn, hdc2tog, hdc in each st to last st, 2 hdc in last st.

Row 2: Ch 2 (does not count as a st), turn, 2 hdc in first st, hdc in each st to last 2 sts, hdc2tog.

Rep Rows 1 and 2 until longest straight edge measures about 19" (48.5 cm).

Decrease Section

Rows 1-13: Ch 2 (does not count as a st), turn, hdc2tog, hdc in each st to last 2 sts, hdc2tog – 4 hdc at the end of Row 13.

Row 14: Ch 2 (does not count as a st), turn, (hdc2tog) twice – 2 hdc.

Row 15: Ch 2 (does not count as a st), turn, hdc2tog – 1 hdc.

Fasten off, leaving a long yarn tail for sewing. Use yarn tail to sew short ends of piece together.

Band

Note: Band is worked back and forth in rows and is joined to Hat at the end of every other row.

From RS, with smaller hook, working around one open end of Hat, join yarn with a sl st in end of first row following the Hat seam.

Set up Rnd: Ch 1, work an even number of sc evenly spaced around edge of Hat; join with sl st in first sc.

Row 1: Ch 8, sc in 2nd ch from hook and in each ch across; sl st into next sc on edge of Hat – 7 sc.

Row 2: Sl st into next sc on edge of Hat, turn, working in back loops only, sc in each st across.

Row 3: Ch 1, turn, working in back loops only, sc in each st across; sl st into next sc on edge of Hat.

Rep Rows 2 and 3 until band has been worked all the way around edge of Hat, end with a Row 2 as the last row you work.

Fasten off, leaving a long yarn tail for sewing. Sew ends of band together.

FINISHING

Thread blunt needle with a doubled strand of yarn. Weave needle in and out through spaces at ends of rows around end of Hat opposite band. Pull ends of strand to close top of Hat and knot. From wrong side, sew any openings at top of Hat closed.

Weave in ends.

WRISTERS (make 2)

With larger hook, ch 3.

Increase Section

Row 1: Work 2 hdc in 3rd ch from hook (2 skipped ch do not count as a st) – you will have 2 hdc in this row.

Row 2: Ch 2 (does not count as a st), turn, 2 hdc in each st – 4 hdc.

Rows 3-9: Ch 2 (does not count as a st), turn, 2 hdc in first st, hdc in each st to last st, 2 hdc in last st – 18 hdc at the end of Row 9.

Center Section

Row 1: Ch 2 (does not count as a st), turn, hdc2tog, hdc in each st to last st, 2 hdc in last st.

Row 2: Ch 2 (does not count as a st), turn, 2 hdc in first st, hdc in each st to last 2 sts, hdc2tog.

Rep Rows 1 and 2 until longest straight edge measures about 8" (20.5 cm).

Decrease Section

Rows 1-7: Ch 2 (does not count as a st), turn, hdc2tog, hdc in each st to last 2 sts, hdc2tog – 4 hdc at the end of Row 7.

Row 8: Ch 2 (does not count as a st), turn, (hdc2tog) twice – 2 hdc.

Row 9: Ch 2 (does not count as a st), turn, hdc2tog – 1 hdc.

Fasten off, leaving a long yarn tail for sewing. Sew short ends of piece together, leaving an opening for thumb.

Cuff

Note: Cuff is worked back and forth in rows and is joined to wrist edge at end of every other row.

From RS, with smaller hook, join yarn with sl st in end of first row following seam.

Set-up Rnd: Ch 1, work an even number of sc evenly spaced around edge of Wrister; join with sl st in first sc.

Row 1: Ch 8, sc in 2nd ch from hook and in each ch across; sl st into next sc on edge of Wrister – 7 sc.

Row 2: Sl st into next sc on edge of Hat, turn, working in back loops only, sc in each st across.

Row 3: Ch 1, turn, working in back loops only, sc in each st across; sl st into next sc on edge of Hat.

Rep Rows 2 and 3 until Cuff has been worked all the way around edge of Wrister, end with a Row 2 as the last row you work.

Fasten off, leaving a long yarn tail for sewing. Use yarn tail to sew ends of cuff together.

FINISHING

Weave in ends.

tilted blocks cowl

◼◼◻◻◻ **EASY**

Shown on page 9.

SIZE

Finished Circumference:
About 45" (114.5 cm)
Finished Height:
About 8" (20.5 cm)

SHOPPING LIST

Yarn (Medium Weight)
LION BRAND® LANDSCAPES®
(Art. #545)
- ☐ #202 Mountain Range -
  1 ball (A)
- ☐ #204 Desert Spring -
  1 ball (B)
  or colors of your choice

Crochet Hook
LION BRAND® crochet hook
- ☐ Size K-10.5 (6.5 mm)
  or size needed for gauge

Additional Supply
- ☐ LION BRAND® large-eyed
  blunt needle

GAUGE

3 blocks = about 4½" (11.5 cm).
BE SURE TO CHECK YOUR GAUGE.

NOTES

1. Cowl is worked in one piece, beginning with a foundation row, then joining to work in the round.
2. Starting with a Foundation Row makes it easier to join on Rnd 1 without twisting.
3. Yarn color is changed on every round.
4. To change yarn color, insert hook into stitch indicated. Yarn over with new color and draw through all loops on hook to complete the stitch. Proceed with new color. Carry color not in use up wrong side of the Cowl.

COWL

With A, and leaving a long yarn tail, ch 211.

Foundation Row: With A, work 3 dc in 4th ch from hook (3 skipped ch count as dc – first block made), sk next 3 ch, sc in next ch, *ch 3, dc in next 3 ch (block made), sk next 3 ch, sc in next ch; rep from * across – you will have 30 blocks at the end of this row.

Join to work in the round

With B, and being careful not to twist, join with sl st in ch-3 sp of first block.

Rnd 1: With B, ch 3 (counts as first dc), turn, 3 dc in first sc (first block made), *sk next 3 dc, (sc, ch 3, 3 dc) in next ch-3 sp (block made); rep from * around, sc in top of beg ch, change to A in last st and join with sl st in turning ch.

Rnd 2: With A, rep Rnd 1, change to B in last st and join with sl st in turning ch.

Rnds 3-10: Rep Rnds 1 and 2.

Rnd 11: Rep Rnd 1.
Fasten off.

FINISHING

With beginning yarn tail, sew ends of Foundation Row together.

Weave in yarn ends.

rainbow strip scarf

▮▭▭▭ BEGINNER

SIZE
About 8" x 54" (20.5 cm x 137 cm)

SHOPPING LIST

Yarn (Medium Weight) 📶4
LION BRAND® LANDSCAPES®
(Art. #545)
- ☐ #201 Boardwalk - 3 balls
  or color of your choice

Crochet Hook
LION BRAND® crochet hook
- ☐ Size K-10.5 (6.5 mm)
  or size needed for gauge

Additional Supply
- ☐ LION BRAND® large-eyed
  blunt needle

GAUGE
11 hdc = about 4" (10 cm).
BE SURE TO CHECK YOUR GAUGE.

NOTE
We sewed our strips at 2 or 3
points for approximately 2"
(5 cm) at each point, leaving long
openings between the strips.

STRIP I (make 2)
Ch 151.

Row 1: Hdc in 3rd ch from hook
(counts as first hdc) and in each ch
across – 150 hdc.

Rows 2 and 3: Ch 2 (count as first
hdc), turn, hdc in each st across.
Fasten off.

STRIP II (make 3)
Ch 6.

Row 1: Hdc in 3rd ch from hook
(counts as first hdc) and in each ch
across – 5 hdc.

Row 2: Ch 2 (counts as first hdc), turn, hdc in each st across.

Rep Row 2 until the piece measures about 54" (137 cm) from beginning. Fasten off.

FINISHING
Lay the strips side by side onto a flat surface, alternating Strips I and II. Sew the strips together at random points to make the Scarf. Weave in ends.

bella vista shawl

■■□□ **EASY +**

Shown on page 15.

SIZE
About 22" x 53"
(56 cm x 134.5 cm) at longest and widest points

SHOPPING LIST

Yarn (Medium Weight) 🧶4
LION BRAND® LANDSCAPES® (Art. #545)
☐ #204 Desert Spring - 3 balls **or** color of your choice

Crochet Hook
LION BRAND® crochet hook
☐ Size K-10.5 (6.5 mm) **or** size needed for gauge

Additional Supply
☐ LION BRAND® large-eyed blunt needle

GAUGE
3 V-sts + 7 rows = about 4" (10 cm).
BE SURE TO CHECK YOUR GAUGE.

STITCH GUIDE
V-STITCH (abbreviated V-St)
(Dc, ch 1, dc) in indicated st or sp.

NOTES
1. Shawl is worked in one piece beginning at lower point.
2. For those who find a visual helpful, we've included a stitch diagram.

SHAWL
Ch 6.

Row 1: V-st in 5th ch from hook, dc in last ch – you will have 1 beg ch-sp, 1 V-st, and 1 dc at the end of this row.

Row 2: Ch 6, turn, V-st in 5th ch from hook, sk next V-st, (sl st, ch 3, V-st, dc) in beg ch-sp – 2 V-sts.

Row 3: Ch 6, turn, V-st in 5th ch from hook, sk next V-st, (sl st, ch 3, V-st) in next ch-3 sp, sk next V-st, (sl st, ch 3, V-st, dc) in beg ch-sp – 3 V-sts.

Row 4: Ch 6, turn, V-st in 5th ch from hook, *sk next V-st, (sl st, ch 3, V-st) in next ch-3 sp; rep from * once more, sk last V-st, (sl st, ch 3, V-st, dc) in beg ch-sp – 4 V-sts.

Rows 5-38: Ch 6, turn, V-st in 5th ch from hook, *sk next V-st, (sl st, ch 3, V-st) in next ch-3 sp; rep from * to last V-st, sk last V-st, (sl st, ch 3, V-st, dc) in beg ch-sp – 38 V-sts at the end of Row 38.
Fasten off.

FINISHING
Weave in ends.

reduced sample of pattern stitch
(repeat Row 5, working one more V-st
in each row, for a total of 38 rows)

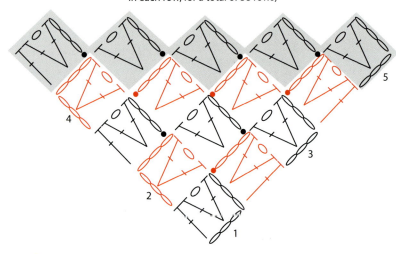

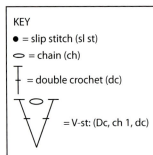

KEY
● = slip stitch (sl st)
◠ = chain (ch)
┼ = double crochet (dc)
V = V-st: (Dc, ch 1, dc)

chocolate ripple poncho

■■□□ EASY

SIZE

About 20" x 52" (51 cm x 132 cm), before folding

SHOPPING LIST

Yarn (Medium Weight) 4
LION BRAND® LANDSCAPES®
(Art. #545)
☐ #203 Sand Dune - 6 balls
   or color of your choice

Crochet Hook
LION BRAND® crochet hook
☐ Size K-10.5 (6.5 mm)
   or size needed for gauge

Additional Supplies
☐ LION BRAND® stitch markers
☐ LION BRAND® large-eyed
   blunt needle

GAUGE

1 ripple = about 4" (10 cm)
measured from peak to peak.
BE SURE TO CHECK YOUR GAUGE.

STITCH GUIDE

DOUBLE CROCHET 2 TOGETHER (abbreviated dc2tog) (uses 2 sts) (Yarn over, insert hook in next st and draw up a loop, yarn over and draw through 2 loops) twice, yarn over and draw through all 3 loops on hook – 1 st decreased.

NOTES

1. Poncho is made from a rectangle worked in a ripple pattern.
2. The rectangle is folded, then 2 edges are crocheted together leaving an opening to make the neck.
3. A border is crocheted around the neck and the outside edges of the Poncho.
4. This project is worked in a ripple crochet pattern. The ripple pattern is easy to do, but it's important to remember that you may need to work several rows before the ripple pattern becomes clear.

5. The ripple in this design is created by working (dc2tog) twice to form "valleys" and working (2 dc in each of next 2 sts) to form "peaks". In each row, take care to work (dc2tog) twice over each "valley" and (2 dc in each of next 2 sts) in the 2 sts at center of each "peak."
6. For those who find a visual helpful, we've included a stitch diagram.

PONCHO
Ch 63.

Row 1: Dc in 4th ch from hook (3 skipped ch count as first dc), dc in next 3 ch, (dc2tog) twice, dc in next 3 ch, *2 dc in in each of next 2 ch, dc in next 3 ch, (dc2tog) twice, dc in next 3 ch; rep from * to last ch, 2 dc in last ch – at the end of Row 1 you will have 5 ripples.

Row 2: Ch 3 (counts as dc), turn, dc in first st, dc in next 3 sts, (dc2tog) twice, dc in next 3 sts, *2 dc in each of next 2 sts, dc in next 3 sts, (dc2tog) twice, dc in next 3 sts; rep from * to beg ch, 2 dc in top of beg ch.

Rep Row 2 until piece measures about 52" (132 cm) from beg. Do not fasten off.

Edging
Ch 1, turn, sc in each st to last st, 3 sc in last st; work sc evenly spaced along one long side of rectangle to next corner; working in opposite side of foundation ch, 3 sc in first ch, sc in each ch across to next corner.
Fasten off.

FINISHING
Following diagram, fold piece in half to measure about 20" x 26" (51 cm x 66 cm).
Place a marker on the 26" (66 cm) side that does not have an edging, 11" (28 cm) from fold.
Join yarn with a sl st at unfolded end of piece. Work sc evenly spaced through both thicknesses up to marker to join this edge. Beg at marker, work sc evenly spaced around open edge for neck.
Fasten off.

Weave in ends.

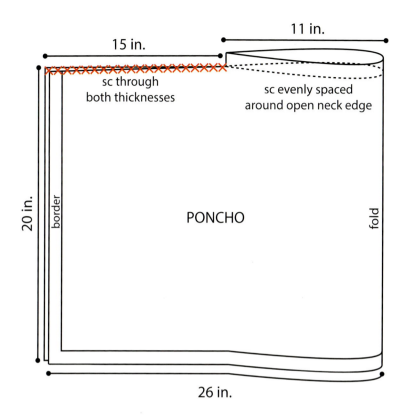

11 in.

15 in.

20 in.

border

sc through
both thicknesses

sc evenly spaced
around open neck edge

PONCHO

fold

26 in.

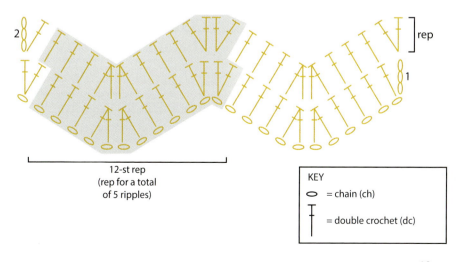

2

rep

1

12-st rep
(rep for a total
of 5 ripples)

KEY

$\circ$ = chain (ch)

$\dagger$ = double crochet (dc)

springdale cowl

EASY +

SIZE
Finished Circumference:
About 55" (139.5 cm)
Finished Height: About 7" (18 cm)

SHOPPING LIST

Yarn (Medium Weight)
LION BRAND® LANDSCAPES®
(Art. #545)
☐ #202 Mountain Range -
2 balls
or color of your choice

Crochet Hook
LION BRAND® crochet hook
☐ Size K-10.5 (6.5 mm)
or size needed for gauge

Additional Supply
☐ LION BRAND® large-eyed
blunt needle

GAUGE
10 hdc = about 4" (10 cm).
BE SURE TO CHECK YOUR GAUGE.

STITCH GUIDE
**HALF DOUBLE CROCHET
2 TOGETHER (abbreviated
hdc2tog)**
(Yarn over, insert hook in next st
and draw up a loop) twice, yarn
over and draw through all 5 loops
on hook – 1 st decreased.

NOTES
1. Cowl is made from 12 triangles,
   working sts across previous
   triangle to begin the next and
   following a diagram.
2. Ends of piece are sewn together
   to make a ring, then an edging
   is worked around the outside
   edges of the Cowl.

COWL
Triangle I
Ch 24.

Row 1 (RS): Sc in 2nd ch from
hook and in each sc across – 23 sc.

Row 2: Ch 3 (counts as hdc, ch 1),
turn, sk next st, hdc in next st,
*ch 1, sk next st, hdc in next st;
rep from * across – 12 hdc and
11 ch-1 sps.

Row 3 (Decrease Row): Ch 2 (counts as first hdc in this row and in all following rows), turn, working in back loops only, yarn over, insert hook in first ch-1 sp and draw up a loop, yarn over, insert hook in next hdc and draw up a loop, yarn over and draw through all 5 loops on hook, hdc in each ch-1 sp and hdc to last st before turning ch-sp, yarn over, insert hook in last st before turning ch-sp and draw up a loop, yarn over, insert hook in 2nd ch of turning ch and draw up a loop, yarn over and draw through all 5 loops on hook – 21 sts.

Row 4 (Decrease Row): Ch 2, turn, working in both loops, hdc2tog, hdc in each st to last 3 sts, hdc2tog, hdc in last st (top of turning ch) – 19 sts.

Row 5 (Decrease Row): Ch 2, turn, working in back loops only, hdc2tog, hdc in each st to last 3 sts, hdc2tog; working in both loops, hdc in last st – 17 sts.

Rows 6-13: Rep Rows 2-5 twice – 5 sts at the end of Row 13.

Row 14: Ch 3 (counts as hdc, ch 1), turn, sk next st, hdc in next st, ch 1, sk next st, hdc in last st – 3 hdc and 2 ch-1 sps.

Row 15: Ch 2, turn, working in back loops only, yarn over, insert hook in first ch-1 sp and draw up a loop, yarn over, insert hook in next hdc and draw up a loop, yarn over, insert hook in next ch-1 sp and draw up a loop, yarn over and draw through all 7 loops on hook; working in both loops, hdc in last st – 3 sts.

Row 16: Ch 1, turn, sk first 2 sts, sc in top of turning ch – 1 st. Do not fasten off.

Triangle II
Row 1 (RS): Ch 1, turn, work 23 sc evenly spaced across side edge of Triangle I – 23 sc.

Rows 2-16: Work same as Rows 2-16 of Triangle I. Do not fasten off.

Triangle III
Row 1 (RS): Ch 1, turn, work 23 sc evenly spaced across side edge of Triangle II – 23 sc.

Rows 2-16: Work same as Rows 2-16 of Triangle I.
Fasten off.

Triangle IV
Row 1 (RS): From RS, and following diagram, join yarn with sl st in corner of previous Triangle to work across side edge, ch 1, work 23 sc evenly spaced across side edge – 23 sc.

Rows 2-16: Work same as Rows 2-16 of Triangle I.
Do not fasten off.

Triangle V
Row 1 (RS): Ch 1, turn, work 23 sc evenly spaced across side edge of previous Triangle – 23 sc.

Rows 2-16: Work same as Rows 2-16 of Triangle I.
Fasten off.

Triangles VI-XI
Rep Triangles IV and V three more times.

Triangle XII
Rep Triangle IV.
Fasten off.

FINISHING
Sew ends of piece together to make a ring.

Edging
From RS, join yarn with sl st at either end of seam.

Ch 1, working evenly along outside edge of piece, work (sc, ch 1) around; join with sl st in first sc.
Fasten off.

Repeat edging around opposite edge of Cowl.

Weave in ends.

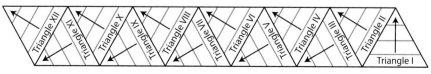

peabody hat and mitts

SIZES

Hat
Finished Circumference:
About 19" (48.5 cm), will stretch to fit a range of sizes
Finished Height: About 9" (23 cm)
Mitts
Finished Circumference:
About 9" (23 cm), will stretch to fit a range of sizes
Finished Length: About 9" (23 cm)

SHOPPING LIST

Yarn (Medium Weight) **④**
LION BRAND® LANDSCAPES®
(Art. #545)
☐ #206 Metropolis - 2 balls
or color of your choice

Crochet Hook
LION BRAND® crochet hook
☐ Size J-10 (6 mm)
or size needed for gauge

Additional Supply
☐ LION BRAND® large-eyed blunt needle

GAUGE
12 hdc = about 4" (10 cm).
BE SURE TO CHECK YOUR GAUGE.

NOTES
1. Both Hat and Mitts are each made in 2 halves.
2. The halves are sewn together following diagrams.

HAT
Half (make 2)
Ch 30.

Row 1: Hdc in 3rd ch from hook (2 skipped ch do not count as a st), and in each ch across - you will have 28 hdc.

Row 2: Ch 2 (does not count as a st), turn, hdc in each st across.

Rows 3-22: Repeat Row 2.
Fasten off.

FINISHING

Following diagram, sew sides of Halves together along one side, then sew remaining sides together to make a tube.

Thread yarn into blunt needle and weave in and out of sts around one open end of tube.

Pull yarn to gather, then knot for top of Hat.

MITTS
First Half (make 2)

Ch 30.

Row 1: Repeat Row 1 of Hat.

Rows 2-9: Repeat Row 2 of Hat. Fasten off.

Second Half (make 2)

Ch 14.

Row 1: Hdc in 3rd ch from hook (2 skipped ch do not count as a st), and in each ch across – you will have 12 hdc.

Rows 2-22: Repeat Row 2 of Hat. Fasten off.

FINISHING

Following diagram, sew sides of First and Second Halves together along one side.

Sew remaining sides together, leaving an opening for thumb. Weave in ends.

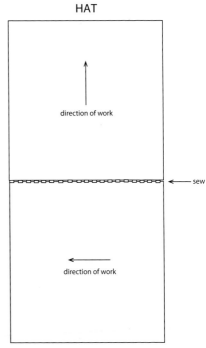

HAT

direction of work

sew

direction of work

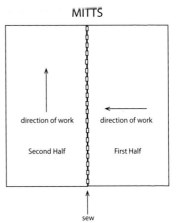

MITTS

direction of work

direction of work

Second Half

First Half

sew

hot springs hat and scarf

■■□□ **EASY**

SIZES
Hat
Finished Circumference:
About 18" (45.5 cm), will stretch to fit a range of sizes
Scarf
About 7" x 60" (18 cm x 152.5 cm)

SHOPPING LIST

Yarn (Medium Weight) **4**
LION BRAND® LANDSCAPES®
(Art. #545)
- ☐ #200 Tropics - 4 balls
  or color of your choice

Crochet Hook
LION BRAND® crochet hook
- ☐ Size K-10.5 (6.5 mm)
  or size needed for gauge

Additional Supplies
- ☐ LION BRAND® stitch markers
- ☐ LION BRAND® large-eyed blunt needle

GAUGE
12 sc = about 4" (10 cm).
BE SURE TO CHECK YOUR GAUGE.

STITCH GUIDE
SINGLE CROCHET 2 TOGETHER (abbreviated sc2tog)
(Insert hook in next st and draw up a loop) twice, yarn over and draw through all 3 loops on hook – 1 st decreased.

NOTES
1. Hat Rib is worked back and forth in rows, then sts are worked along one edge of rib and Hat is worked in the round.
2. Scarf Rib is worked same as Hat Rib, then sts are worked along one edge to work length of Scarf.
3. A second rib section is worked and slip stitched to end of Scarf.

HAT
Rib
Ch 9.

Row 1: Sc in 2nd ch from hook and in each ch across – 8 sc.

Row 2: Ch 1, turn, working in back loops only, sc in each st across.

Rep Row 2 until piece measures about 18"(45.5 cm) from beg, unstretched.
Do not fasten off.

Body
Rnd 1 (RS): Working across long side edge of ribbing, ch 1, work 56 sc evenly spaced across; join with sl st in first sc.
Place marker for beg of rnd; move marker up as each rnd is completed.

Rnd 2: Ch 2 (counts as hdc), hdc in next st and in each st around.

Rnd 3: Hdc in each st around.

Rep Rnd 3 until piece measures about 8" (20.5 cm) from beg.

Shape Crown (top of Hat)
Rnd 1: *Sc in next 2 sts, sc2tog; rep from * around – you will have 42 sc.

Rnd 2: *Sc in next st, sc2tog; rep from * around – 28 sc.

Rnd 3: Sc2tog around – 14 sc.
Fasten off, leaving a long yarn tail.

Thread tail through sts of Rnd 3 and pull to gather. Knot securely.

FINISHING
Sew short ends of Hat Rib together.

Weave in ends.

SCARF
Beginning Rib
Ch 16.

Row 1: Sc in 2nd ch from hook and in each ch across – 15 sc.

Row 2: Ch 1, turn, working in back loops only, sc in each st across.

Rows 3-24: Rep Row 2.
Do not fasten off.

Body

Row 1 (RS): Working across long side edge of rib, ch 1, work 22 sc evenly spaced across.

Row 2: Ch 2 (counts as first hdc), turn, hdc in next st and in each st across.

Rep Row 2 until piece measures about 56" (142 cm) from beg. Fasten off.

Ending Rib

Make same as Beginning Rib. Fasten off.

With WS together, slip stitch Ending Rib to last row of Scarf.

FINISHING

Weave in ends.

sunset shrug

EASY +

SHOPPING LIST

Yarn (Medium Weight)
LION BRAND® LANDSCAPES®
(Art. #545)
- ☐ #204 Desert Spring -
  5{6} balls
  or color of your choice

Crochet Hook
LION BRAND® crochet hook
- ☐ Size K-10.5 (6.5 mm)
  or size needed for gauge

Additional Supplies
- ☐ LION BRAND® stitch markers
- ☐ LION BRAND® large-eyed
  blunt needle

SIZES
S/M{L/1X}
Finished Width:
About 37½{42½}"/95.5{108} cm
Finished Length:
About 25{27}"/63.5{68.5} cm,
before folding and seaming
Note: Pattern is written for smaller
size with changes for larger size in
braces. When only one number is
given, it applies to both sizes. To
follow pattern more easily, circle
all numbers pertaining to your
size before beginning.

GAUGE
10 sts + 9 rows = about 4" (10 cm)
over (sc, dc) pattern of Row 2.
BE SURE TO CHECK YOUR GAUGE.

NOTES
1. Shrug is worked in one piece,
   then folded and seamed.
2. A diagram is provided to clarify
   construction.

SHRUG

Ch 95{107}.

Row 1 (RS): Sc in 2nd ch from hook, *dc in next ch, sc in next ch; rep from * to last ch, dc in last ch – 94{106} sts.

Rows 2-54{58}: Ch 1, turn, sc in first dc, *dc in next sc, sc in next dc; rep from * to last sc, dc in last sc.

Last Row (Top Edging): Ch 1, turn, sc in each st across.
Fasten off.

FINISHING
Lower Edging

From RS and working across opposite side of foundation ch, join yarn with sc in ch at base of first st; work sc in each ch across.
Fasten off.

Sleeve Edging

Row 1: From RS, join yarn with sc at beg of one side edge. Working in ends of rows, sc evenly spaced across edge.

Row 2: Ch 1, turn, sc in each st across.
Fasten off.

Rep edging across opposite side edge.

Following diagram, fold piece in half. Place markers on edge (not on fold), 9" (23 cm) from side edges for sleeves. Sew or slip stitch each edge together between corner and marker.

Weave in ends.

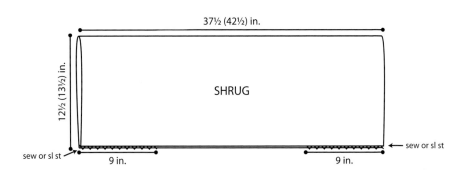

37½ (42½) in.

12½ (13½) in.

SHRUG

sew or sl st

9 in.

sew or sl st

9 in.

blocks and dots scarf

■■□□ **EASY**

SIZE
About 12" x 58" (30.5 cm x 147.5 cm)

GAUGE
Three 3-dc groups = about 4" (10 cm).
BE SURE TO CHECK YOUR GAUGE.

SHOPPING LIST

Yarn (Medium Weight) 🔵4
LION BRAND® LANDSCAPES® (Art. #545)
- ☐ #206 Metropolis - 2 balls (A)
- ☐ #200 Tropics - 1 ball (B)

  or colors of your choice

Crochet Hook
LION BRAND® crochet hook
- ☐ Size J-10 (6 mm)

  or size needed for gauge

Additional Supplies
- ☐ LION BRAND® stitch markers (optional)
- ☐ LION BRAND® large-eyed blunt needle

NOTES
1. Scarf is worked in one piece.
2. The yarn color is changed on every row but piece is only turned on every other row. Follow the pattern carefully and turn piece only when instructed.
3. When changing the yarn color, drop, but do not cut, the old color. Carry color not in use up side of piece until next needed.

4. Because the piece is only turned on every other row, the yarn color is changed using different methods for A and for B.
   a. To change to A, work last st of B to last yarn over. Drop B. Return dropped loop of A to hook and draw through all loops to complete the last st. Turn the piece and proceed with A.
   b. To change to B, remove the loop of A from hook and enlarge it or place it on a stitch marker or safety pin so that it does not unravel. Do not turn the piece. Return to beg of row just completed, insert hook in top of beg ch, yarn over with dropped strand of B and draw up a loop. Proceed with B.
5. For those who find a visual helpful, we've included a stitch diagram.

SCARF

With A, ch 39.

Row 1 (RS): Dc in 4th ch from hook (3 skipped ch count as first dc), dc in next 2 ch, *ch 1, sk next ch, dc in next 3 ch; rep from * to last 5 ch, ch 1, sk next ch, dc in last 4 ch – you will have one 4-dc group at the beg and end of this row, seven 3-dc groups between the 4-dc groups, and 8 ch-1 sps. Remove loop of A from hook and enlarge it or place it on a stitch marker or safety pin so that it does not unravel.

Row 2 (RS): From RS, insert hook in top of beg ch; leaving a long beg tail to weave in later, draw up a loop of B, ch 1, sc in top of same beg ch, *ch 3, sk next 3 dc, sc in next ch-1 sp; rep from * to last 4 dc, ch 3, sk next 3 dc, sc in last dc and change to A – 10 sc and 9 ch-3 sps. Drop but do not cut B.

Row 3 (WS): With A, ch 3 (counts as dc), TURN, 3 dc in first ch-3 sp, *ch 1, sk next sc, 3 dc in next ch-3 sp; rep from * to last sc, dc in last sc. Remove loop of A from hook and enlarge it or place it on a stitch marker or safety pin so that it does not unravel.

Row 4 (WS): From WS, insert hook in top of beg ch, pick up dropped strand of B and draw up a loop, ch 1, sc in top of same beg ch, *ch 3, sk next 3 dc, sc in next ch-1 sp; rep from * to last 4 dc, ch 3, sk next 3 dc, sc in last dc and change to A.

Row 5 (RS): With A, ch 3 (counts as dc), TURN, 3 dc in first ch-3 sp, *ch 1, sk next sc, 3 dc in next ch-3 sp; rep from * across, dc in last sc. Remove loop of A from hook and enlarge it or place it on a stitch marker or safety pin so that it does not unravel.

Row 6 (RS): From RS, insert hook in top of beg ch, pick up dropped strand of B and draw up a loop, ch 1, sc in top of beg ch, *ch 3, sk next 3 dc, sc in next ch-1 sp; rep from * to last 4 dc, ch 3, sk next 3 dc, sc in last dc and change to A – 10 sc and 9 ch-3 sps. Drop but do not cut B.

Rep Rows 3-6 until piece measures about 58" (147.5 cm) from beg, end with a Row 3 or Row 5 as the last row you work.
Fasten off.

FINISHING
Weave in ends.

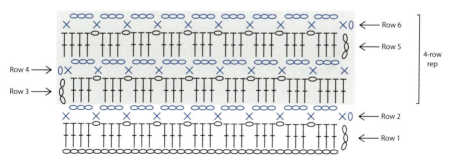

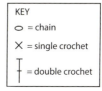

KEY

○ = chain

✕ = single crochet

┬ = double crochet

fan lace vest

EASY +

SHOPPING LIST

Yarn (Medium Weight) 4
LION BRAND® LANDSCAPES®
(Art. #545)
- ☐ #204 Desert Spring -
  4{6} balls
  or color of your choice

Crochet Hook
LION BRAND® crochet hook
- ☐ Size J-10 (6 mm)
  or size needed for gauge

Additional Supplies
- ☐ LION BRAND® stitch markers
- ☐ LION BRAND® large-eyed
  blunt needle

SIZES
Women's {Plus}

Finished Back Width:
About 25{30}"/63.5{76} cm
Finished Back Length:
About 25{30}"/63.5{76} cm
Note: Pattern is written for smaller size with changes for larger size in braces. When only one number is given, it applies to both sizes. To follow pattern more easily, circle all numbers pertaining to your size before beginning.

GAUGE
2 pattern reps = about 3½" (9 cm) in Fan Lace pattern.
Note: On RS rows one pattern rep consists of one 4-dc group and the following ch-3 sp. On WS rows one pattern rep consists of one sc and the following ch-7 sp.
BE SURE TO CHECK YOUR GAUGE.

PATTERN STITCH

Fan Lace Pattern
(foundation ch is multiple of 8 ch + 2 additional ch)

Row 1 (RS): Sc in 2nd ch from hook, *sk next 3 ch, 4 dc in next ch, ch 3, sk next 3 ch, sc in next ch; rep from * across.

Row 2: Ch 6 (counts as dc, ch 3), turn, sk first ch-3 sp, sc in first dc (first dc of first 4-dc group), *ch 7, sk next ch-3 sp, sc in first dc of next 4-dc group; rep from * to last 4 sts, ch 3, sk next 3 dc, dc in last sc.

Row 3: Ch 1, turn, sc in first dc, sk next ch-3 sp, 4 dc in next sc, *ch 3, sc in next ch-7 sp, 4 dc in next sc; rep from * to beg ch-6, ch 3, sc in 3rd ch of beg ch-6.

Rep Rows 2 and 3 for Fan Lace pattern.

NOTES

1. Vest is made in one piece, then folded and seamed following a diagram.
2. Back is worked first, then fronts are worked along side edges of back.
3. For those who find a visual helpful, we've included a stitch diagram.

VEST

Back

Beg at top edge of Back, ch 114{138}.

Beg with Row 1 of pattern, work in Fan Lace pattern until piece measures about 25{30}"/63.5{76} cm from beg – you will have 14{17} pattern reps in each row.
Fasten off.

Place a marker on each side edge about 10½{14}"/26.5{35.5} cm from Row 1.

Left Front

Hold Back with RS facing you and Row 1 at top.

Row 1 (RS): From RS, join yarn with sc in top left corner of Back, work (4 dc, ch 3, sc) 6{8} times evenly spaced along edge to marker – 6{8} pattern reps. Remove marker.

Beg with Row 2 of pattern, work in Fan Lace pattern for 14½{16}"/37{40.5} cm.
Fasten off.

Right Front

Hold Back with RS facing you and Row 1 at top.

Row 1 (RS): From RS, join yarn with sc in right side edge of Back at marker, work (4 dc, ch 3, sc) 6{8} times evenly spaced along edge to top right corner – 6{8} pattern reps. Remove marker.

Beg with Row 2 of pattern, work in Fan Lace pattern for 14½{16}"/37{40.5} cm. Fasten off.

Front Edging

From RS, join yarn with sc in lower right front corner, work (4 dc, ch 3, sc) 8{9} times evenly spaced along right front edge working a 9th{10th} 4-dc group in join between right front and back, ch 3, work sc, (4 dc, ch 3, sc) 13{16} times evenly spaced along back neck edge working a 14th{17th} 4-dc group in join between back and left front, ch 3, work sc, (4 dc, ch 3, sc) 8{9} times evenly spaced along left front edge – 31{36} pattern reps. Fasten off.

Weave in ends.

FINISHING

Fold fronts over back, bringing top edges of fronts to center front. Sew about 4{4½}"/10{11.5} cm of front side edges (A) to back side edges (B) following diagram on page 44, leaving openings for armholes.

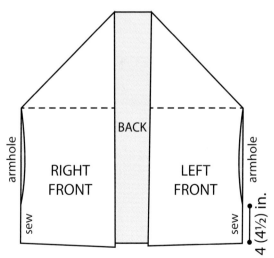

43

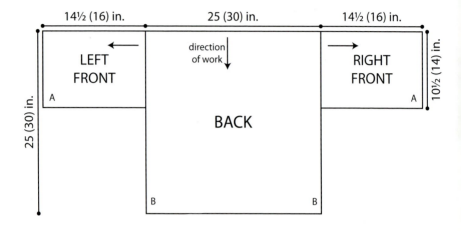

14½ (16) in.   25 (30) in.   14½ (16) in.

LEFT FRONT

direction of work

RIGHT FRONT

10½ (14) in.

A

A

25 (30) in.

BACK

B   B

Fan Lace Pattern
(reduced sample)

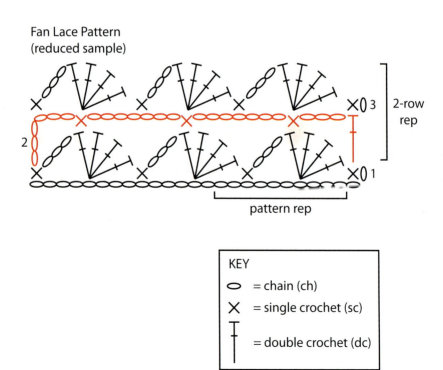

2-row rep

pattern rep

KEY

⬭	= chain (ch)
✕	= single crochet (sc)
┰	= double crochet (dc)

general instructions

ABBREVIATIONS

beg = begin(ning)(s)
ch = chain
ch-sp(s) = chain space (s)
  previously made
cm = centimeters
dc = double crochet
hdc = half double crochet
mm = millimeters
rem = remain(ing)(s)
rep(s) = repeat(s)
RS = right side
rnd(s) = round(s)
sc = single crochet
sk = skip
sl st = slip stitch
sp(s) = space(s)
st(s) = stitch(es)
tog = together
WS = wrong side

* — When you see an asterisk used within a pattern row, the symbol indicates that later you will be told to repeat a portion of the instruction. Most often the instructions will say, repeat from * so many times.

( ) or [ ] — Sets off a short number of stitches that are repeated or indicates additional information.

– When you see – (dash) followed by a number of stitches, this tells you how many stitches you will have at the end of a row or round.

GAUGE

Never underestimate the importance of gauge. Achieving the correct gauge assures that the finished size of your piece matches the finished size given in the pattern.

CROCHET TERMINOLOGY		
UNITED STATES		INTERNATIONAL
slip stitch (slip st)	=	single crochet (sc)
single crochet (sc)	=	double crochet (dc)
half double crochet (hdc)	=	half treble crochet (htr)
double crochet (dc)	=	treble crochet (tr)
treble crochet (tr)	=	double treble crochet (dtr)
double treble crochet (dtr)	=	triple treble crochet (ttr)
triple treble crochet (tr tr)	=	quadruple treble crochet (qtr)
skip	=	miss

CHECKING YOUR GAUGE

Work a swatch that is at least 4" (10 cm) square. Use the suggested hook size and the number of stitches given. If your swatch is larger than 4" (10 cm), you need to work it again using a smaller hook; if it is smaller than 4" (10 cm), try it with a larger hook. This might require a swatch or two to get the exact gauge given in the pattern.

METRICS

As a handy reference, keep in mind that 1 ounce = approximately 28 grams and 1" = 2.5 centimeters.

CROCHET HOOKS																
U.S.	B-1	C-2	D-3	E-4	F-5	G-6	7	H-8	I-9	J-10	K-10½	L-11	M/N-13	N/P-15	P/Q	Q	S
Metric - mm	2.25	2.75	3.25	3.5	3.75	4	4.5	5	5.5	6	6.5	8	9	10	15	16	19

◼◻◻◻ BEGINNER	Projects for first-time crocheters using basic stitches. Minimal shaping.	
◼◼◻◻ EASY	Projects using yarn with basic stitches, repetitive stitch patterns, simple color changes, and simple shaping and finishing.	
◼◼◼◻ INTERMEDIATE	Projects using a variety of techniques, such as basic lace patterns or color patterns, mid-level shaping and finishing.	
◼◼◼◼ EXPERIENCED	Projects with intricate stitch patterns, techniques and dimension, such as non-repeating patterns, multi-color techniques, fine threads, small hooks, detailed shaping and refined finishing.	

Yarn Weight Symbol & Names	LACE (0)	SUPER FINE (1)	FINE (2)	LIGHT (3)	MEDIUM (4)	BULKY (5)	SUPER BULKY (6)	JUMBO (7)
Type of Yarns in Category	Fingering, size 10 crochet thread	Sock, Fingering, Baby	Sport, Baby	DK, Light Worsted	Worsted, Afghan, Aran	Chunky, Craft, Rug	Super Bulky, Roving	Jumbo, Roving
Crochet Gauge* Ranges in Single Crochet to 4" (10 cm)	32-42 sts**	21-32 sts	16-20 sts	12-17 sts	11-14 sts	8-11 sts	6-9 sts	5 sts and fewer
Advised Hook Size Range	Steel*** 6 to 8, Regular hook B-1	B-1 to E-4	E-4 to 7	7 to I-9	I-9 to K-10½	K-10½ to M/N-13	M/N-13 to Q	Q and larger

*GUIDELINES ONLY: The chart above reflects the most commonly used gauges and hook sizes for specific yarn categories.

** Lace weight yarns are usually crocheted with larger hooks to create lacy openwork patterns. Accordingly, a gauge range is difficult to determine. Always follow the gauge stated in your pattern.

*** Steel crochet hooks are sized differently from regular hooks–the higher the number, the smaller the hook, which is the reverse of regular hook sizing.

TERMS

fasten off — To end your piece, you need to simply cut and pull the yarn through the last loop left on the hook. This keeps the last stitch intact and prevents the work from unraveling.

right side — Refers to the front of the piece.

LION BRAND® LANDSCAPES®

Article #545
Weight Category: 4 - Medium
Weight: Fashion and accessories
Solids & Self-Striping: 3.5oz/100g (147yd/134m)
Fiber Content: 100% Acrylic

Gauge:
Knit: 16.5 sts x 22 rows on size 10 (6.5 mm) needles
Crochet: 12 sc x 15 rows on K-10.5 (6.5 mm) hook

Product Care Instructions:

Items made from this yarn may be machine laundered only on the setting designed for gentle agitation and/or reduced time for delicate items. Any dry cleaning solvent other than trichloroethylene may be safely used. No bleach product may be used. Item may not be machine dried; instead lay flat to dry. Item may not be smoothed or finished with an iron.

VISIT LionBrand.com FOR:
• Learn to Knit & Crochet Instructions
• Weekly newsletter with articles, tips, and updates
• Store Locator

We have made every effort to ensure that these instructions are accurate and complete. We cannot, however, be responsible for human error, typographical mistakes, or variations in individual work.